Ethics for Trustees 2.0

A Guide for All Who Serve as Trustee

Marguerite C. Lorenz, CTFA, CLPF

ABSTRACT

This guideline is for everyone who needs to select a Successor Trustee, and for everyone who serves as a Trustee of a Trust; experienced or inexperienced; Attorneys, Fiduciaries, CPA's, Family Members and Friends, etc. Quotes and concepts have been drawn from personal experience based on serving as private professional trustees in California.

authorHOUSE®

AuthorHouse™
1663 Liberty Drive
Bloomington, IN 47403
www.authorhouse.com
Phone: 833-262-8899

Published by AuthorHouse 09/24/2020

ISBN: 978-1-7283-7278-5 (sc)
ISBN: 978-1-6655-0201-6 (e)

Library of Congress Control Number: 2020918922

Print information available on the last page.

This book is dedicated to my partners and staff. Thank you for all that you do to serve our clients so well!

With Love, Marguerite

Contents

Foreword

10 YEARS AGO, WHEN THE first edition of this book was written, I wrote the forward as a brand-new fiduciary. I was a young CPA who decided to get into the fiduciary industry after I was invited to join a long-time practice with my mother, Jane Lorenz, and my sister, Marguerite Lorenz. A lot has changed in our practice and the industry, but not a lot has changed in my opinion of the profession, and the importance of this book and a good mentor. When I first started, I did not know that the professional would require such discipline and commitment to serious principles, and over time I have learned how often those principles are challenged and tested.

The reason I was willing to try a new profession with which I had so little previous experience or knowledge, was that I knew I had mentors with this experience to share. The importance of this book and mentors comes with the wide variety of issues we face as Fiduciaries. Without help, how would you know the many traps that await a trustee? How would you know how to avoid all the conflict that is rife within every decision? How would you even know how to start and who to go to for help and support for your clients?

Licensing is an important development in the growth of our profession, but many professionals are exempt from this process.

CPAs, Attorneys and Broker Dealers/Investment Advisors can act as a Professional Fiduciary without obtaining a license. Within our own firm, we have two licensed attorneys and a licensed CPA. We are all exempt from licensing but we have all pursued Fiduciary Licenses because we should be held to the same standards that all Professional Fiduciaries are held.

The estate planning industry is not young itself, but the many niche careers within it are young and blossoming. The education and training within these niches is therefore difficult to come by. Licensing for fiduciaries offers this opportunity, shows all interested parties that a licensed individual has sought training, and adheres to the principles for which the Professional Fiduciaries Bureau has set forth. A young, inexperienced professional does not have the experience to show potential clients and referrers, so they must do anything they can to earn their trust.

Jane and Marguerite bring many years of successful experience to this book, and they are helping the industry as a whole by sharing that experience and understanding of the profession. Jane passed away in 2017, though her memories, training and love carry on with everyone she touched over her 30+ years in this industry. There are so many difficult decisions a trustee will encounter, and this book will help to prepare any professional or amateur to better approach them. Anyone reading this has demonstrated their desire to learn more, and to be the best trustee they can be. The reader clearly wants to learn how to see the traps and conflicts before or when they arrive, so I applaud you for making this effort. I hope that this profession will grow and earn the respect that it deserves because of all the honorable, principled professionals that make it up.

The professional Fiduciary, by definition, must provide the HIGHEST standard of care, must be equitable, fair and honest. Ethics are within each of us, and different to each of us, but the specific situations and specific standards within an industry, like estate planning, are not inherently known to the average person. That is why this book needed to be written, and why it can provide value to even the most experienced professional fiduciary, anyone considering serving as a trustee or executor even once, and everyone who must select a successor to serve them.

When I was still very new to our company, our office received a gift from a service provider that appeared to be more than $50 in value. I looked at this beautiful gift and recommended that we graciously return it, because it did not seem free of conflict. It was not a commission or a bribe, but a thoughtful thank you. The appearance of conflict was there, however, and it did not seem worth the risk. It is amazing that I saw this first, considering it was from my mentor's training that I had viewed the situation this way, but that goes to show how important it is to have other ethical individuals around you. It shows how great my mentor's reinforced their ideas of ethics and conflict of interest into my training. Impropriety is not a part of my life, and it shouldn't be a part of anyone's life in this industry, but I was told from the very beginning, that it has to go deeper than that.

The color of impropriety needs to be avoided. We not only need to be ethical but we need to give the onlooker no reason to believe we represent anything but the highest standard of moral principles. We are given trust like no other professional and if we are to be given the respect and position in the world that we hope to achieve, then we must embody these principles and prove beyond any reasonable doubt that we deserve that trust.

Clay B. Spiegel, CPA, CLPF #608

Second Edition - Introduction

JANE B. LORENZ, CPA, CLPF had been practicing as a CPA since 1975 and started serving as a Professional Trustee in the late 1980's. Marguerite C. Lorenz, CTFA, CLPF began working with Jane in 2003 and has been serving as a Professional Trustee ever since.

Jane passed away in 2017. The first book was written as partners, and this second edition is a labor of love, as Jane (Stepmom) and Marguerite (Stepdaughter) had a special family and business partnership. Updating this book is a great way to honor Jane, while bringing the book to current regarding laws that have changed and Marguerite's additional experience since the first publication.

We know the challenges facing today's Fiduciary, whether amateur or professional. We know many professional Fiduciaries operate as solo practitioners, without partners or staff. We have benefitted so much from our partnership and business model; we feel good about sharing some of what we have learned.

Since the first edition came out in 2011, our company has grown to five trustees, and with offices in Southern California (Los Angeles, Orange, Riverside and San Diego Counties) and New Hampshire. We see that the fiduciary profession has enjoyed more awareness, but California is still the only state licensing its fiduciaries, and it has since 2007. This book is designed to stimulate discussion in our estate planning community, to emphasize the value of continuing education, and to encourage those who serve as a Fiduciary to do their best.

Jane had served as President of the Professional Fiduciary Association of California (PFAC), had served as a Commissioner on the Estate Planning Law Advisory Commission, and until her untimely passing, mentored new PFAC board members. Jane had been writing articles, and educating through public speaking, throughout her entire career. She is greatly missed by her family, her work team, her clients, and her colleagues.

Marguerite has spoken at several professional conferences on the topic of Ethics for Attorneys and Fiduciaries. She is President of the Estate Planning Group Network (EstatePlanningGroups.com). She has served as Chairman of the Professional Fiduciaries Bureau Advisory Committee (Department of Consumer Affairs), having been nominated by Governor Brown in 2012. Marguerite is Vice Chair for the Independent Trustee Alliance (TrusteeAlliance.com), and she continues to be a thought leader on LinkedIn (https://www.linkedin.com/in/californiatrustee/), and other social media platforms.

Marguerite is a Master Trustee and continues to inspire Estate Planning professionals, in all related industries, who all serve the same vulnerable clientele.

Jane and Marguerite co-authored the first edition of this book. All new items were authored by Marguerite alone. Since some the book was derived from Jane's personal experience, much of the wisdom she contributed is still here. This book is filled with Jane and/or Marguerite's opinions, based on their experiences as professional trustees and is not to be construed as legal advice. All rights are reserved and owned by Lorenz Fiduciary Services, Inc.

The word "Fiduciary" can refer to Professionals and Amateurs, as the focus is on the role and its duties, performed by anyone over the age of 18 who has been named in an estate plan.

We strongly recommend that you seek the services of a licensed attorney, preferably one who specializes in Estate Planning, Trusts,

Wills and Probate matters. The guidance here can help make your own estate plan more effective for you and your loved ones.

This book is not a "How to" and is offered as a reference guide, not as a sole source or guidance in the work as trustee. We suggest that you gain a working knowledge of the Probate Code, take Fiduciary Management classes and develop good administration skills before taking on the role of Trustee. For those considering a career change, we also strongly suggest that you consider how you will acquire your first case, <u>before</u> embarking on the challenging road of being a Professional Fiduciary.

Your feedback and comments are welcome! You can write to us at:

EthicsForTrustees@MyTrustee.net

Chapter 1
Is this a new profession?

IT HAS BEEN SAID THAT the law of trusts developed in the Middle Ages from the time of the Crusades (around 1100 to 1275) under the jurisdiction of the King of England. This has been known as the original and foundational law of trusts in the world, and a unique contribution to our "Common Law".

Trusts are part of the law of property, and arise where one person (a "settlor", or "trustor") gives assets (e.g. some land) to another person (a "trustee") to keep safe or to manage on behalf of another person (a "beneficiary"). Think Employer/Employee; Trustor/Trustee. This arrangement creates a Fiduciary relationship between the trustee and the beneficiary. For the benefit of the non-professionals who read this book, we offer the following basic information and summary.

Fiduciary (Fi-dū-shē-airy): The word itself comes originally from the Latin **fides**, meaning faith, and **fiducia**, trust. A Fiduciary (this can be anyone given the job, i.e., a family member, a professional, an institution, etc.) is expected to be extremely loyal to the person(s) to whom he owes the duty (the "trustor", the "beneficiary"): **he must not put his personal interests before the duty**, and must not profit from his position as a Fiduciary, unless the principal consents.

"Profit", in this instance, may mean "take advantage of" or "experience gain beyond any agreed upon reasonable compensation". Corporate Fiduciaries, as well as Private Fiduciaries often make it a practice to fully disclose fees, in a published schedule. This disclosed amount, discussed ahead of time with the Trustor allows the Trustor to decide what is reasonable. Family and Friend trustees don't have such a schedule and may choose not to be paid, at first.

Typically, the work of Trust Administration takes many more hours and is considerably more stressful than the Trustor, Family member or Friend realized. Stressed Family and Friends are doubly challenged to keep to their ethical compass, if they are expected to do this work without pay. Resentments often build and create additional tension, when no compensation for this work was considered or drafted into the estate plan.

As you accept the role of Trustee, how you will be compensated is an important discussion to have with the Trustor. We acknowledge this information may be obvious to professionals, but needs to be highlighted and discussed for the benefit of our amateur readers who wish to "do the job right". Whether or not you are paid, it is appropriate to track your time, document your activities and accurately track every transaction. You will make better decisions as the Trustee, if you are also managing the resources to get the job done.

A Trust involves the administration of assets on behalf of another: an institution or one or more individuals, living or dead. A Trustee can be appointed to manage assets during the lifetime of the original settlor; this private arrangement allows for distribution of wealth even if the client becomes incapacitated, or is unable to act personally. Upon death of the settlor or trustor, the trust controls how and when assets are used and distributed; this is not the same as a court appointment of a legal guardian or conservator (also Fiduciary capacities) to handle assets inherited by young children or others unable to act on their own behalf, although a trust can be set up to benefit those same individuals under a guardianship or conservatorship (this depends on the Probate Code in your state). We intend to focus on the ethical issues experienced by trustees of trusts, not on those issues managed by conservators or guardians, although there is a natural overlap.

By bypassing the probate process through which a will is handled by the judicial system, a trust may reduce costs or delays, allow for immediate medical care for the surviving spouse, manage real estate, provide more privacy than a bequest in a will, and offer possible tax advantages. In order for these advantages to benefit the trust, not only does the document need to be well drafted, the individual who serves as trustee must be a good manager who knows what questions to ask.

We believe there have been Fiduciary relationships as long as there have been people and property.

At the primary level, this relationship can be described as a "position of trust." In the last few hundreds of years, various individuals, mainly lawyers, have acted in the Fiduciary capacity.

As a licensed profession, it is quite new. The Professional Fiduciary Association of California was organized in 1995 as a combination of three regional groups. In Northern California there was the California Association of Professional Conservators and Fiduciaries, in Los Angeles there was the Professional Conservators of Southern California, and in San Diego there was the Professional Fiduciary Association.

In 2003 an affiliation was formed between PFAC and the National Guardianship Association to offer more support and educational opportunities. Whether you are a well-meaning family member, a close friend, attorney, CPA (or you are planning to be a Professional Fiduciary), we strongly recommend that you pursue formal training and licensing. There are Certificates being offered currently at Cal State Fullerton and at University of California, Riverside, as of this writing.

In 2016, the Independent Trustee Alliance, a non-profit association, was started to meet the needs of trustees (professional and amateur) around the world. Initial Board members included active Independent Trustees, attorneys, and other professionals who believe in ethical practice of this important work. Members are supported with offerings of group health insurance, accessible liability insurance, and access to continuing education included in the nominal cost of membership. Learn more at TrusteeAlliance.com.

Speaking from an ethics standpoint, we believe you can fulfill your duties more effectively, and take better care of yourself, if you acquire focused fiduciary training. We feel that being licensed as a Fiduciary means that you are willing to be held accountable for your work. It is our understanding that attorneys and CPA's have no on point training and their licensing exams do not cover anything about serving as the Trustee of a Trust. Ethics requirements are different for different professions and do not necessarily cover the same duty of loyalty to the client as the Fiduciary ethic. The insurance coverage for an attorney or CPA does not necessarily cover work as a Fiduciary, either.

About the First Trustee of the Trust...

Please note that the Trustor has a responsibility to "think through" the management of the Trust, once the Trustor is no longer able to manage alone, in light of incapacity, resignation and death.

If you are serving as Trustee for another's Trust, consider having an estate plan of your own. When we speak, we often ask the audience members to raise their hands if they have a complete estate plan, updated in the last 3-5 years. We are continually surprised how many professionals do not have a complete estate plan of their own, especially those with businesses that would suffer if there was an abrupt change without a plan to handle it.

We recommend getting your own plan done, before you serve on anyone else's trust. You will understand the depth of the decisions, the hope of the intentions and the ultimate goals much more effectively having had to come to terms with your own wishes.

Clearly, it is not just the documents as drafted, but as much the individual charged with the responsibility, which makes the difference in how a trust is administered. We feel this falls under Ethics for Trustees, as typically, the Trustor is also the first Trustee of the Trust. Please read Chapter 16, Ethics in Action, for more on this.

Chapter 2
Who is choosing this profession?

I N THE FIRST TEN YEARS of the Professional Fiduciary Association of California (PFAC), it seemed clear that two groups of older, experienced people were choosing this profession of becoming a Fiduciary. Professionals from fields such as social work and medicine were choosing to become Conservators, which is very "people oriented" work. Professionals from accounting, law, tax and investment backgrounds were choosing to become Trustee, which is "financially oriented "work.

Young people were less present to this career choice. Becoming a Fiduciary was a career that seemed to require significant life experience and self-confidence. Often, a person who served a family member realized that they enjoyed the work and took it on professionally for non-family members.

We believe the following three events have contributed to the growth of our profession:

1) The internet made it easier to for people to find this opportunity.

2) Cal State Fullerton developed a certificate program for Trustees, and one for Conservators. PFAC members served on their Advisory Board.
3) Licensing became required in 2008 (PFAC had been working toward licensing since it was founded).

Now, there was a clear career path at a time when many people were re-inventing themselves (due to major changes in our economy). Younger people began to take an interest in this profession, which up to this point had been mainly older professionals from related fields. The financial crisis of 2008 made some professionals rethink their careers, and a few found being a professional fiduciary to be a fresh start.

Since we have met so many who are new to this profession, we felt an open discussion of Ethics for Trustees was needed. At this writing, there are about 700 California Licensed Professional Fiduciaries. More than 100 of these licensees do not serve as fiduciaries, but instead, have acquired the designation as a marketing enhancement. Not all licensees are members of PFAC or the Independent Trustee Alliance (ITA). Not all professionals (and certainly not amateur family members) who serve as Fiduciaries are licensed or insured as Fiduciaries (Note: In addition to other professionals, CPA's, Attorneys and Bank Trust Officers are **exempt** from licensing).

With so many who serve as Trustees without a license and without supportive membership, we feel it is important for professionals and consumers to be educated on these ethical issues as well. Perhaps some family breakups, financial disasters and financial elder abuse can be prevented if more information is available about what to expect from one's chosen Fiduciary.

Chapter 3
Licensing in California

T HE PROFESSIONAL FIDUCIARIES BUREAU WAS created by legislation that passed and was enacted into law in 2007 to regulate non-family member professional fiduciaries, including conservators, guardians, trustees, and agents under durable power of attorney as defined by the Professional Fiduciaries Act. An Attorney was appointed the chief of the Bureau and the Governor appointed 7 members to an advisory committee. The Bureau chief hired a staff of four and went to work. Regulations were promulgated.

The Bureau was designed to be a self-funding organization and it was assumed that 800 individuals would apply for licensing, since there were more than that listed on the statewide registry at the time. Since that is a fairly small group, the application fee was $400 and the initial annual license fee was set at $600. The annual renewal fee was $700. It is our understanding that these fees were higher than those for attorneys and for CPAs in California. Fees have increased since then. Licensing fees have continued to increase over the years.

Previous to the licensing legislation, the State of California had a statewide registry that listed the credentials of professional fiduciaries and all professionals who served as Fiduciaries. There were approximately 1500 such professionals listed, who were fingerprinted and background checked by the California Department of Justice, before the statewide registry was discontinued. There was no minimum education or experience required but any credentials claimed by the individual were verified by the state. There was a fee, in addition to the initial expense of fingerprinting/lifescan, charged every 3 years for this service.

In addition, each county had its own procedure in place for registering professional fiduciaries. The forms requested information regarding court supervised cases and assets under management.

Within a year or so, it became apparent to the Chief of the Bureau that the original expectation of 800 applicants was not accurate. Keep in mind, many of whom used to be on the statewide registry were now exempt, so that meant that the Bureau budget would not balance. There would not be sufficient fee income to support the chief and staff of four.

Unfortunately, in our opinion, the following individuals are <u>not required to obtain a license</u>:

1) a trust company or employee
2) an FDIC-insured institution or employee
3) a public officer or public agency
4) a broker-dealer and investment advisor
5) an attorney
6) a CPA
7) an enrolled agent

Within a few years, the Bureau chief had resigned and the staff was reduced to one half time person. Members of the California State Bar expressed their concern that the courts would grind to a halt because the required licenses would not be processed.

By the end of 2010, the Bureau staff was replenished and the licensing and renewal procedures were working again. At this writing, the Bureau continues to function, and has a full complement of advisory committee members.

The initial licensing application and the renewal forms were simple for inexperienced applicants, and more challenging for more experienced applicants. The Bureau required the disclosure of all cases, court supervised or not, which had ever been worked. For a Professional Fiduciary with 20 years of experience, this required a great deal of time, reviewing old files and listing those cases.

Questions also required disclosure regarding the conclusion of all those cases, whether distributed and terminated or transferred to another Fiduciary or discharged in any manner. As far as we know, *none of the professions exempted from Fiduciary licensing are required to disclose any cases they have worked on to renew, or initiate, their professional licenses.* A professional who is licensed as a Fiduciary is held to a higher standard, has more responsibility and is scrutinized more carefully than other professionals who are not licensed Fiduciaries. When Jane died, her license information was reconciled, and her record marked as Deceased. Whenever a California licensed fiduciary retires, a reconciliation is also required.

The training and experience that is necessary to properly fulfill the role of a professional trustee is not automatically available to a person with the above licenses or professions. When Jane began working as a trustee (after working as a CPA for 15 years), there was no "on point" fiduciary training available. In more recent years, there is more adequate on-point education and mentoring, which can significantly accelerate competence. We have taught, and learned much, in our professional community.

We have been asked many times if an attorney or CPA should be licensed as a Fiduciary, when the law says they are exempt. Our answer is Yes, anyone who serves as a Fiduciary, on two or more cases, should be licensed to do so. An attorney recently responded by saying her license is more "stringent" than the Fiduciary license.

We offer that though being an attorney does have its rules, they are not the same and so are not necessarily more stringent than the rules that a Fiduciary must uphold. Each profession has its own "way of being".

Attorneys, CPAs, Doctors and other professionals are essentially "advisors", not the decision makers. When they advise clients, the client can take or leave their advice, at their own peril, of course. When one is the decision maker, all the liability rests with this person. It is a significant and fundamental difference between these professions and being the fiduciary, who does become the decision maker.

Professional is defined as: 1. A person formally certified by a professional body of belonging to a specific profession by virtue of having completed a required course of studies and/or practice and whose competence can usually be measured against an established set of standards. 2. A person who has achieved an acclaimed level of proficiency in a calling or trade.

The root word for Profession is "Profess", to affirm openly; declare or claim. There is a sense of promise in this definition. We believe these concepts of open declaration and promise are carried by everyone who seeks out, goes through the training, performs the testing rituals and carries the license of their profession. Whether a realtor, doctor, attorney, fiduciary, CPA or other licensed profession, we feel that each carries its own ideas of best standards of practice, has its own focus on service to the consumer and has its own forms of protection due to the way the work is carried out.

We would like everyone who isn't "required to be licensed" to consider getting licensed as a Fiduciary anyway because:

1. The license one may have now, as a CPA or attorney, does not include any requirement for on-point training in the role as Fiduciary.
2. The CPA and/or Bar licensing exam did not ask any questions about what one might do in different circumstances as the Fiduciary, another training opportunity lost.

3. The licensing board (of CPA's and/or lawyers) is not reviewing your past or current cases as a Fiduciary, or recording how much you have under management.

4. Without a specific continuing education requirement, we fear that unlicensed practitioners are not taking the time to update their knowledge or improve their standards of practice as Trustees.

5. We did not see a section in the State Bar to support attorneys who serve as trustee.

6. Your malpractice insurance may not cover work as a Fiduciary, as this is well beyond the normal scope of practice with a great deal more liability.

7. The CPA and Attorney Code of Ethics (or Professional Code of Conduct), agreed to by those who are licensed under these professions, are not the same as the Fiduciary Code of Ethics.

8. Being licensed in the profession in which you work denotes to colleagues and the public the higher standards by which you operate.

9. Attorneys and CPAs wish their licenses to continue to be respected and are generally unhappy when an unlicensed professional performs the same services the licensed professionals do. For instance, an attorney who sells audit services, or a CPA who writes estate plans.

10. Not being licensed contributes to the misinformation about estate planning issues much like online "Do It Yourself" estate planning and legal document assistants contribute to clients creating estate plans without informed advice.

Consumers of Fiduciary services should be educated about our licensing process. We are concerned that those individuals who serve as Fiduciaries, without being licensed, who are avoiding the licensing process, may not be educated appropriately in the first place and may not be continuing appropriate education. By definition, a Fiduciary must put the client's interests before his own. We believe that going through this licensing process is a demonstration of willingness to put the client first.

For those professionals who have decided not to be licensed as a Fiduciary, we recommend making sure you have appropriate insurance, as in Errors and Omissions coverage, with your regular business or malpractice carrier, specifically for your work in a Fiduciary capacity.

As for attorneys who draft the same trusts in which they are named as trustees (in our experience very few attorneys do this), or other professionals, such as CPA's or Financial Advisors who draft trusts (but do not have a license to practice law) please consider full disclosure of your lack of appropriate licensing to the unwary client. Given that there is such a strong Fiduciary community, you no longer have to do all the work yourself. The client needs your advocacy, and the client is better served when there is a team approach.

For the non-professional reader: If your attorney and the trustee are one and the same person, who is your advocate (the wise professional in your corner) if the accounting is inaccurate?

Many attorneys do a fine job as the Fiduciary, and if they also drafted the documents, they have had another attorney perform an "independent review" to be sure this arrangement is beneficial to the client and that it is what the client wants. It appears to be a higher ethical road when the attorney who drafts the documents does not also serve under those documents.

Chapter 4
The Judicial System in California

THE SUPERIOR COURT HAS JURISDICTION over the Probate Court in California. Each County has its own courts and judges. The judges hold meetings at least annually and provide continuing education for each other.

The San Diego Court has taken the lead recently in an attempt to add modern computer technology to their system. As is often the case, it has not been easy.

The San Francisco Court system has been a leader in developing legislative guidance for Conservatorships. They requested assistance from local fiduciaries in the development of training for non-professional conservators and made the training a requirement for non-professionals before they were allowed to serve. Professional Fiduciaries in San Francisco, and later in San Diego, volunteered their time to teach the classes.

In 2010 and 2011, as part of the budget difficulties of the State of California, the Probate Court has had to deal with budgetary changes and closures of the court related to "furloughs" to reduce payroll costs. It was not an easy time. In San Diego today, the Bar assists the court in many ways including attorneys giving of their time to serve as judge pro tems and settlement conference judges to help the court with budget shortfalls.

During this time, the awareness that there are professional licensed fiduciaries available has increased. Even our local court has encouraged drafting attorneys to keep professionals in mind when structuring a trust. It has also been strongly suggested that co-trusteeships do not work, except to increase the volume of cases in our courtrooms. We are pleased to know that our judiciary system appreciates our licensing and professionalism.

Chapter 5
The Probate Code

I N CALIFORNIA AND OTHER STATES, the Probate Code is the body of law that governs Fiduciary practice. It has separate sections dealing with Estates, Conservatorships and Trusts. Every state has its own, as we do not yet have a uniform or Federal Probate Code.

A Fiduciary acting as Executor or Administrator in a Probate Estate, or as a Conservator, would by necessity be represented by an attorney. In Trust administration, it has been our policy to always engage the services of a knowledgeable Estate Planning attorney on every matter. Proper completion of the Notice to Heirs and the lodging of the will with the county are requirements in every Estate Settlement. And in every ongoing trust, legal issues arise for which legal advice is appropriate. All of these attorneys work with the Probate Code daily. In addition, the Fiduciary should be knowledgeable of the sections of the law that pertain to his/her practice.

We enjoy the team aspect of working with counsel. We strategize together. We sometimes ask counsel to review our trust accountings, before we send it to the beneficiaries. Although we may be able to accomplish a trust administration without ever going to court, working with an attorney from the beginning of each case is our policy because we never know, as we begin, what may come up. It is more effective to begin with counsel and keep the attorney up to date than it is to get a new attorney up to speed, once issues arise. We have also seen instances where good counsel prevented complications and issues, just by being an effective communicator.

Chapter 6
Professional Associations

Professional Fiduciary Association of California™
Code of Conduct (Revised 2/25/2015)

M EMBERS OF THE PROFESSIONAL FIDUCIARY Association of California should:

- Abide by the Professional Fiduciaries Act (California Business and Professions Code Sections 6500-6592) and the Act's implementing regulations (California Code of Regulations Sections 4400-4622), including the Professional Fiduciaries Bureau Code of Conduct.
- Recognize that the client is the prime responsibility and strive to provide services which reflect respect for each client.
- Not engage in any form of discrimination on the basis of race, color, sex, sexual orientation, age, religion, national origin or any other condition or status.

- Manifest personal integrity, assume responsibility and accountability for individual judgments and maintain an attitude of fairness, honesty, respect, courtesy and good faith in all professional relationships.
- Cooperate with colleagues to promote common professional interests and concerns and facilitate ethical and competent professional performance.
- Seek and maintain competence in professional skills and seek to contribute to the ongoing development of the profession's body of knowledge.

You can find more information at PFAC-pro.org – This California organization provides educational opportunities through its chapter meetings, and annual conferences.

The Independent Trustee Alliance (ITA); Mission Statement, Code of Ethics, and Best Practices:

Mission Statement: ITA will set the standard of care, diligence and professionalism for those who have been named trustee or expect to be named as trustee of a trust or serve in another fiduciary capacity for beneficiaries or families. By adhering to the standards set forth in the ITA Code of Ethics, Statement of Best Practices and other requirements of membership, members strive to perform their fiduciary duties with a high degree of professionalism. Through interaction with other members, educational initiatives and even professional certification ITA allows members to continually improve their skills and remain leaders in the field of independent trust administration.

Code of Ethics:

As Independent Trustees, we acknowledge that we serve a vulnerable population of beneficiaries. We also acknowledge that we have a hope and desire to educate individuals who are laymen and have either been named as trustees or co-trustees who seek to improve their knowledge and competency in accepting and carrying out the responsibilities and duties of Trusteeship.

Trustors/Settlors must rely on trusted individuals to carry out their wishes, and to fulfill their promises to the beneficiaries.

Beneficiaries hope for the fulfillment of the Settlor's promises are in the hands of the Trustee. The Independent Trustee Alliance (ITA) believes that Independent Trustees are the best Individuals to carry out the fulfillment of those wishes and for those reasons have created ITA.

ITA is an organization that interested persons can join to learn the process of performing Trustee duties in a responsible, and ethically appropriate manner, thus serving the best interests of the beneficiaries, to whom they owe their first duty of loyalty. ITA believes that no one should be a member of ITA who has not first agreed to the high standards of professionalism that should guide their conduct as a trustee.

Therefore, ITA sets forth this Code of Ethics for all who wish to join our organization.

DUTY OF LOYALTY: An ITA member must agree to identify the beneficiaries to whom a duty of loyalty is owed; frequently the first beneficiary is the Settlor, who for a variety of reasons is unwilling or not capable of managing the trust assets. The trust instrument also frequently sets out a list of heirs, charities and loved ones, as successor, beneficiaries. All actions taken by the Trustee must be taken in the best interest of those beneficiaries.

CONFLICT OF INTEREST:

    (a) A member of ITA must agree to avoid actual conflicts of interest, and consistent with faithful fiduciary conduct agree not to engage in any activity where there is the reasonable appearance of a conflict of interest.

    (b) An ITA member shall not engage in any personal, business, or professional interest or relationship that is or reasonably could be perceived as self-serving or adverse to the best interest of the persons or entity being served.

(c) The ITA member shall protect the rights of the beneficiaries of the trust against manipulation by third parties.

BEST PRACTICES:

ITA has been formed by a group of professionals who serve as trustees and also provide ancillary services for serving Trustees and those who work in the Trust industry.

The reason the founders came together to form ITA is their desire to set a high bar of professionalism for those who wish to serve as an Independent Trustee, and provide dedicated, faithful service to the beneficiaries they have been asked or appointed to serve.

In addition to the ITA Code of Ethics, the founders have established a set of best practices that all ITA members are expected to follow in the course of their duties as Trustees. Those best practices are as follows:

COMPLIANCE WITH APPLICABLE LAW

The trustee shall comply with all local, state, and federal laws, regulations, and requirements developed by ITA as a minimum guide for the fulfillment of the fiduciary duties.

The trustee shall seek competent professional advice whenever appropriate and in the best interests of the beneficiary.

FEES AND SERVICES

Many members will come from other disciplines such as Law, Accounting, Banking and Financial Services. As an ITA member, when serving as a paid trustee, care must be taken to be sure that fees for services are for work as the trustee and not for additional services (e.g. The drafting attorney must consider carefully if also serving as trustee in the same matter is in the best interest of the settlor and beneficiaries, and then decide on appropriate compensation).

Other professional experience can be important background, adding to the ITA member's ability to perform the work as trustee the exercise of good judgment and the efficient performance of Trustee tasks, but should not be utilized to inflate a trustee's compensation for trust services. The duty of loyalty and absence of conflict of interest should be clear, in all agreements and activities of the ITA member, and in the performance of the ITA member's work as a trustee.

FAITHFUL AND DILIGENT ADMINISTRATION

The ITA member should generally be mindful of the impact of the administration on

1. the beneficiaries,
2. any other stakeholders, and
3. family harmony

and make every effort to help the beneficiaries and the family function in a fashion that carries out the purposes of the trust.

Management of the Trustee's Risk:

*   A trustee shall not compromise his loyalty by acting (or by choosing not to act) solely in order to reduce his personal exposure to liability risk.
*   A trustee shall tend to the management of his own risks as well as that of the trusts he administers.
*   A trustee should be insured.

COMMITMENT TO REGULAR COMMUNICATION WITH THE SETTLOR AND ALL BENEFICIARIES

Providing those whom a trustee serves with accurate and timely information regarding the administration of the trust is at the core of truly appropriate and faithful service by the trustee. The greatest cause of uncertainty, discomfort and fear on the part of beneficiaries is lack of communication to them by the trustee. ITA members when serving as trustee are expected to commit themselves to complete, transparent and timely information on their actions as trustee and proposed changes planned for the administration or operations of the trust.

COMMITMENT TO CONTINUED EDUCATION AND
THE IMPROVEMENT OF PROFESSIONALISM

ITA members are encouraged to continue to improve their knowledge and skills, through attending CE offerings, sharing ideas and information with colleagues and assisting them in their professional development.

Those who wish to raise their level of Professionalism above the level of Regular Membership are encouraged to apply for and attain accreditation as a Certified Independent Trustee®, through the ITA program for certification of Independent Trustees.

DUTY OF CARE

One of the primary fiduciary duties required of a trustee is the duty of care to the beneficiaries served by the trustee. The duty of care requires the trustee to make decisions after taking all available information into account and then taking action that will be faithful to the purposes of the trust and in the best interest of the beneficiaries.

Trustees are required to exercise the utmost care in making decisions in order to fulfill their fiduciary duty.

This national non-profit association offers member benefits such as, an annual conference, access to group health insurance, access to liability insurance, a certification process, and online continuing education is included in membership.

∞

There is currently no specific regulation or oversight that we know of for beneficiaries who also serve as the Trustee. Professional

Fiduciaries are held to a higher standard than amateur family members.

Please explore and study the two sets of regulations found in California Business and Professions Code Sections 6500-6592, known as the "Professional Fiduciaries Act" effective January 1, 2007, and the California Code of Regulations Sections 4400-4622.

Section 6501 (f, 1, A) defines the term of Professional Fiduciary to mean:

A person who acts as a guardian or conservator of the person, the estate, or the person and estate, for two or more individuals at the same time who are not related to the professional fiduciary or to each other.

(B) A personal representative of a decedent's estate, as defined in Section 58 of the Probate Code, for two or more individuals at the same time who are not related to the professional fiduciary or to each other.

(2) "Professional fiduciary" also means a person who acts as a trustee, agent under a durable power of attorney for health care, or agent under a durable power of attorney for finances, for more than three individuals, at the same time.

Chapter 7
The Fiduciary Bureau Code of Ethics

THE DEPARTMENT OF CONSUMER AFFAIRS, Professional Fiduciaries Bureau can be found at: http://www.Fiduciary.CA.gov/

Quoted from the above website: "The Professional Fiduciaries Bureau was created by legislation that passed and was enacted into law in 2007 to regulate non-family member professional fiduciaries, including conservators, guardians, trustees, and agents under durable power of attorney as defined by the Professional Fiduciaries Act. 'Are You A Professional Fiduciary?'" As of this 2nd Edition, The Professional Fiduciaries Bureau has issued more than 1,000 licenses.

Professional fiduciaries provide critical services to seniors, disabled persons, and children. They manage matters for clients including daily care, housing and medical needs, and also offer financial management services ranging from basic bill paying to estate and investment management. Requirements for licensing include passing an examination and completing thirty (30) hours of approved education courses (See Pre-Licensing Education

Information), and earning fifteen (15) hours of continuing education credit each year for renewal. Licensees must comply with reporting requirements and must abide by the Professional Fiduciaries Code of Ethics so that client matters are handled responsibly and without conflict."

See California, Title 16.

Professional and Vocational Regulations

Division 41. Professional Fiduciaries Bureau

Article 4. Code of Ethics.

California Code of Regulations Sections 4470 – 4484 These sections discuss the relationship between the Licensed Fiduciary (the Licensee) and the client. We have taken the following text directly from the California Code of Regulations. The following is not to be construed as legal advice. Rather, we wanted to make it easy for you to refer to these sections as part of our discussion on ethics for trustees.

Article 4. Code of Ethics Section 4470. General Principles.
(a) A licensee's Fiduciary duties recognized under this Article are based upon the Fiduciary relationship established with the consumer as follows:
   (1) A licensee's relationship to a conservatee when acting as a court appointed conservator;
   (2) A licensee's relationship to a ward when acting as a court appointed guardian;
   (3) A licensee's relationship to a principal when acting under a durable power of attorney; and,
   (4) A licensee's relationship to a beneficiary when acting as a trustee.
(b) The licensee shall comply with all local, state, and federal laws and regulations, and requirements developed by the courts and the Judicial Council as a minimum guide for the fulfillment of the Fiduciary duties recognized under this Article.

(c) The licensee shall protect all rights of the consumer that relate to licensee's Fiduciary duties to the consumer.

(d) The licensee shall refrain from representing the consumer in areas outside the scope of legal authority.

(e) The licensee shall seek competent professional advice whenever appropriate for the benefit of the consumer.

(f) Consistent with the licensee's fiduciary duties, the licensee shall provide or arrange for services to the consumer, to the extent they are appropriate and reasonable based upon the needs of the consumer, that are in the best interest of the consumer.

(g) Notwithstanding any other provision of law, any expense incurred by the licensee for the delivery of services that are provided to, or arranged for, the consumer by the licensee, including attorney fees or fees to the licensee for services, shall be considered reasonable if approved by the court.

Note: Authority cited: Sections 6517 and 6520, Business and Professions Code. Reference: Section 6520, Business and Professions Code.

Section 4472. Decision Standards.

(a) The provisions under this section apply to those licensed fiduciaries acting in the capacity of a conservator, guardian, or agent under durable power of attorney for health care or for finances.

(b) The licensee shall provide the consumer with every reasonable opportunity to exercise those individual choices that the consumer is capable of exercising.

(c) When the licensee is making decisions on behalf of the consumer, the licensee shall use every reasonable good faith effort to ascertain the desires of the consumer prior to making any decisions, and shall make decisions therefore predicated on the ascertained desires of the consumer, unless doing so would violate the licensee's Fiduciary duties to the consumer or impose an unreasonable expense on the estate.

(d) If after every reasonable good faith effort the desires of the consumer cannot be ascertained or if exercising them would violate the licensee's Fiduciary duties to the consumer or impose an unreasonable expense on the estate, the licensee shall make decisions that are in the best interest of the consumer.

(e) Decisions made on behalf of the consumer shall take into consideration all known ethnic, religious, social and cultural values of the consumer whenever possible.

Section 4474. Confidentiality.

(a) The licensee shall closely guard against the disclosure of personal information regarding the consumer except when such disclosure is required by law or necessary to protect the best interest of the consumer.

(b) Disclosure of consumer information shall be limited to what is lawful, necessary and relevant to the issue being addressed.

Section 4476. Conflict of Interest.

(a) The licensee shall avoid actual conflicts of interest, and consistent with the licensee's Fiduciary duties, shall not engage in any activity where there is the reasonable appearance of a conflict of interest.

(b) The licensee shall not engage in any personal, business, or professional interest or relationship that is or reasonably could be perceived as self-serving or adverse to the best interest of the consumer.

(c) The licensee shall protect the rights of the consumer and the estate against infringement by third parties.

Section 4478. Residential Placement.

(a) The provisions under this section apply to those licensed fiduciaries acting in the capacity of a conservator, guardian, or agent under durable power of attorney for health care.

(b) The licensee shall be informed and aware, and consider the options and alternatives available when establishing the consumer's place of residence.

(c) The licensee shall use every reasonable good faith effort to ascertain the desires of the consumer prior to making any decisions when establishing the consumer's residence, unless doing so would violate the licensee's Fiduciary duties to the consumer or impose an unreasonable expense on the estate.

(d) If after every reasonable good faith effort the desires of the cannot be ascertained or if exercising them would violate the licensee's Fiduciary duties to the consumer or impose an unreasonable expense on the estate, the licensee shall select the least restrictive and appropriate residence that is available and necessary to meet the needs of the consumer that are in the best interest of the consumer.

(e) The licensee shall not remove the consumer from his or her home or separate the consumer from family and friends unless such removal is appropriate and in the best interest of the consumer.

(f) The licensee shall seek professional evaluations and assessments whenever appropriate to determine whether the current or proposed placement of the consumer represents the least restrictive and appropriate residence that is available and necessary to meet the needs of the consumer that are in the best interest of the consumer.

(g) The licensee shall monitor the placement of the consumer on an on-going basis to ensure its continued appropriateness, and shall make changes whenever necessary that are in the best interest of the consumer.

(h) The licensee shall take all action necessary to protect the consumer from financial and/or physical harm or abuse.

Marguerite C. Lorenz, CTFA, CLPF

Section 4480. Care, Treatment and Services.

(a) The provisions under this section apply to those licensed fiduciaries acting in the capacity of a conservator, guardian, or agent under durable power of attorney for health care.

(b) The licensee shall protect the personal and pecuniary interests of the consumer.

(c) The licensee shall use every reasonable good faith effort to ascertain the desires of the consumer prior to making any decisions regarding all care, treatment, or services, unless doing so would violate the licensee's Fiduciary duties to the consumer or impose an unreasonable expense on the estate.

(d) If after every reasonable good faith effort the desires of the consumer cannot be ascertained or if exercising them would violate the licensee's Fiduciary duties to the consumer or impose an unreasonable expense on the estate, the licensee shall make decisions regarding care, treatment, and services that are in the best interest of the consumer.

(e) The licensee shall be cognizant of his or her own limitations of knowledge, and shall seek professional evaluations and assessments whenever appropriate to determine whether the current or proposed care, treatment, and services are appropriate and in the best interest of the consumer.

(f) The licensee shall monitor the care, treatment, and services on an on-going basis to ensure its continued appropriateness, and shall make changes whenever necessary that are in the best interest of the consumer.

Section 4482. Management of the Estate.

(a) The licensee shall protect the assets of the estate.

(b) The licensee shall pursue claims against others when it reasonably appears to be in the best interest of the consumer or the estate to do so.

(c) The licensee shall defend against actions or claims against the estate when it reasonably appears to be in the best interest of the consumer or the estate to do so.

(d) The licensee may incur expenses that are appropriate to the estate, in relation to the assets, overall investment strategy, purpose, and other relevant information and circumstances when investing and managing estate assets.

(e) Consistent with the licensee's Fiduciary duties, the licensee shall manage the assets of the estate in the best interest of the consumer.

(f) The licensee shall manage the estate with prudence, care and judgment, maintaining detailed Fiduciary records as required by law.

Section 4484. Limitation or Elimination of Fiduciary Powers; Restoration of Capacity; Termination of Fiduciary Relationship.

(a) When appropriate and in the best interest of the conservatee, licensed conservators under the Act shall not oppose and, in appropriate circumstances shall seek, limitations on the licensee's powers or authority to act, elimination of unnecessary or no-longer necessary powers, or termination of the proceeding and restoration of the conservatee's legal capacity.

(b) In all Fiduciary relationships subject to the Act, when appropriate and in the best interest of the consumer, the licensee shall take all reasonable steps to facilitate termination of the Fiduciary relationship.

(c) In all Fiduciary relationships subject to the Act, the licensee shall not oppose or interfere with efforts to terminate the licensee's Fiduciary relationship with a consumer for any reason other than as necessary or appropriate to protect or promote the best interest of that consumer.

NOTE: Authority cited: Sections 6517 and 6520, Business and Professions Code. Section 6520, Business and Professions Code.

Chapter 8
National Guardianship Association

THE NATIONAL GUARDIANSHIP ASSOCIATION (NGA) has the purpose of providing leadership and education for guardians. Please note that in California, the term "Guardian" is specific to the care of a minor, and "Conservator" is specific to the care of adults and is the term used in California which most closely matches the term "Guardian" used in other states.

The Center for Guardianship Certification, a related entity, has developed the skills and procedures for testing professionals. The organization offers two designations: National Registered Guardian and National Master Guardian which require certain experience and success with the related examination. In 2003, the NGA approached PFAC with the invitation to become affiliated. A few other states had developed professional organizations for fiduciaries but PFAC had accomplished more than most. Of course, each state has its own probate code. In addition to testing procedures, NGA also offered visibility into the National scene, including active lobbying in Washington on subjects related to Fiduciary practice. PFAC accepted the offer of affiliation.

After the affiliation, PFAC and NGA worked together to develop testing specifically for California Fiduciaries. PFAC members participated in the testing on a voluntary basis and received the designation of Registered Guardian and Certified Fiduciary upon passing the examination.

When California began requiring licensing of Professional Fiduciaries, the testing discussed above was utilized in the procedures.

The NGA continues to offer training, refresher courses, its own Code of Ethics and an excellent guide on Standards of Practice (most recently updated in 2013). You can learn more at: www.guardianship.org

Chapter 9
Conflicts of Interest

I N SECTION 16004 (A), THE California Probate Code states:
"The trustee has a duty not to use or deal with trust property for the trustee's own profit or for any other purpose unconnected with the trust, nor to take part in any transaction in which the trustee has an interest adverse to the beneficiary."

Two Boys and One Piece of Cake

Two brothers found one last piece of cake. The older offered to cut the cake, and gave the younger the opportunity to select which piece he wanted. Fair, right? This is how it's done in many families. What if the older got to cut the cake, and select which piece he wanted? This situation is not about the character or experience of the older brother. Just having the opportunity to take advantage of the situation creates a conflict of interest.

Untrained Fiduciaries usually have difficulty seeing their own "conflicts of interest." A conflict of interest arises when an action will affect the Fiduciary personally.

For example, if the Fiduciary is also a remainder beneficiary (let's say the eldest son), the Fiduciary will personally benefit (after his Mother passes away) by not spending money on caregivers for the lifetime beneficiary (the Mom). When inheritance occurs, any money spent on Mom will not be there for distribution to the beneficiaries.

The Fiduciary may or may not be fully aware of the conflict because he is emotionally involved, and he may be combating with siblings who have their own priorities. We have heard beneficiaries who serve as trustees tell us, "Mom said not to spend anything extra on her. She wants us to have more to spend after she dies." Mom is the trustor, creator of the trust, and is the first beneficiary of the same trust when she resigns, or is incapacitated. She loves her children, and they love her. She has demonstrated that love by giving her children everything she could. Now, when serving as trustee, her child must put his mother's needs first, above his own. Depending on the family's culture, communication, and expectations, this may be easy or quite difficult.

We have seen cases where the elder can well afford to stay in her home, and she has told everyone of her intention, but never got these specific wishes in writing. Living at home with full time caregivers is rather expensive. Consider that a reputable home care company charges about $30 per hour (It's 2020 and rates vary by availability, geography, skill and quality, especially during a pandemic) hour for a qualified and licensed caregiver. 24 hours at that rate = $720. On a weekly basis that's $5040. Monthly is around $22,000. Annually, full time care can cost about $250,000 (this does not include other living at home expenses such as mortgage, tax, utilities, insurance, groceries, repairs, etc.). She was moved by family members (beneficiaries) to an economical Skilled Nursing Facility ($12,000 monthly) rather than kept at home with 24/7 caregivers, and the home was sold. She cried as she left her home for the last time. She had long term care insurance, but her family member trustee found the paperwork complicated and did not submit a claim.

Many people express a desire to stay at home in their final days, rather than entering an assisted living residence. It is recommended that if there is a very strong desire to remain at home, to discuss this with the drafting attorney with the intention to get this desire stated clearly in the written estate plan, and to consider the alternatives if money is an issue.

To avoid a conflict of interest such as this, it may be necessary to choose a Trustee, and an Agent for Healthcare who are not also beneficiaries. Hospice services are generally paid for by Medicare Coverage and can be extremely helpful in supporting an elder at home (whatever that home environment might be) through the end of life.

The Probate Code, in Section 16002(a) reads: "The trustee has a duty to administer the trust solely in the interest of the beneficiaries." The beneficiary here may be the surviving spouse during her lifetime, while her children are "Remaindermen" (meaning they receive the "Remainder" after her death). In a revocable trust, her children may not be the beneficiaries until she dies, but if it is an irrevocable trust, the trustee may have to answer to the remainder beneficiaries, even while the trustor is still alive. These distinctions lead us to ask, "Who is the client?" in each case. In the situation where a stepchild to the surviving spouse is serving as the Trustee, can the stepchild be expected to administer the trust solely in the interest of his father's spouse?

There are many examples, some obvious and some not so obvious, whereby the Fiduciary is, or appears to be, receiving other compensation.

Let's look at some examples:
1) What if the Fiduciary drives a car owned by the Trust?

Is it to be used just on Trust business, or is it for personal use of the trustee? Is it to "exercise" the car periodically so the battery doesn't die? Is it to drive the lifetime beneficiary somewhere?

So, the conflict here is that the world has no way of knowing the answers to this question. Each person observing the Fiduciary driving the car owned by the Trust will make his or her own decision about the propriety or impropriety of the action. The Fiduciary must have a firm policy about this, preferably in writing.

Ideally, using the car for personal use should never be an option. Some Fiduciaries would choose not to use the car at all, perhaps even to sell it, so there is no doubt about its use.

The Ethical difficulty with this is that there will be some decision points where the choice to avoid a conflict of interest is counter-intuitive. If, for example, the car battery must be charged, wouldn't it be most efficient to do that on Saturday when you have errands to do and your son's soccer game to watch? You might even decide that you won't charge the client for your time since you are getting your own errands done anyway? So that would benefit the Trust, wouldn't it?

Do you see the Ethical dilemma here? The problem is that the Fiduciary is benefiting personally (profiting) by the use of the car and this is in excess of his fees.

And the social impact in your Professional community can be devastating. You will be seen by someone, in a clearly personal environment, using one of your trust's assets. The conclusion they draw will probably not be one of admiring you for your efficiency. Some will consider that you are "stealing" from your client!

So in the example above, the intuitive, efficient answer has to be avoided. The Fiduciary will need to find another way to charge the battery. If the client is being billed on an hourly basis, the Fiduciary will want to consider how to be economical and avoid extra costs to the client. Perhaps there is someone else, a family member or a trusted car maintenance service that can handle this detail. Or perhaps it is time to sell this automobile and provide transportation for the client in other ways. After all, automobile ownership carries a lot of legal liability with it. The Trust might be better off without it!

Another example:

2) What if a Fiduciary transfers money from a trust account into a personal account?

Proper accounting is an affirmative duty of a Fiduciary. We will be discussing internal controls later in this book. Specifically, this is about "mingling" funds. Everyone gets tired, or makes mistakes, or forgets to complete some things. When a Fiduciary doesn't exercise standard procedures, like paying a bill based on an invoice, reconciling the checking account (to be sure the funds are there to pay the bill) and sending the payment in timely fashion, there may be doubt about other payments being made properly.

In our practice, we have separate accounts for each Trust we administer, where a bank or trust company might have a single "operating" account. An individual Fiduciary must never "mingle" funds.

We have seen cases where the responsible party used an ATM card without documentation, or paid a personal bill with trust funds, rather than go through the process of tracking her time and being paid a trustee fee. We feel it is critical that when one serves as a Fiduciary, one must run the Trust as a business, not a hobby. This is where many Family member trustees may blur the distinction between Trust funds and Mom's money, and they have no systems in place to prevent this.

Even when making purchases using the correct financial source, what you purchase needs to be documented appropriately because there may be tax consequences. For instance, medical necessities, such as prescriptions and doctor visits, need to be recorded accurately and reported on tax returns. Tax rules change frequently, and the Fiduciary needs to stay aware of these changes.

If the Fiduciary pays for something "out of pocket" and expects to be reimbursed, documentation is critical. Petty cash needs to be managed as specifically as the checkbook, perhaps more stringently if caregivers are making incidental purchases from this fund.

Bank charges, interest earned and other fees need to be tracked so decisions can be made as to what is best for the client. When Family member trustees are also beneficiaries and become "co-signers" on checking/saving accounts, current expenditures and eventual distributions can become muddied.

We have seen instances where a family member was added

as a co-signer to the trustor's personal checking account to make bill paying "easier" when the trustor becomes too frail to manage independently. What the trustor may not realize is that this personal checking account may have just become accessible to the creditors of the co-signer. When that trustor dies, the money in that account may become the property of the co-signer, without regard to the written estate plan.

Instead, we suggest relying on your written estate plan, and if you are not sure how your plan will actually work (or what you need to do to make sure it will work), ask your attorney more questions, and share the details of all of your assets; how they are titled, who is listed as beneficiary, etc.

Here is an example of how the estate plan goes into action: At the time the trustor becomes too frail to manage, that trustor can resign as trustee. Then the successor trustee, already named in the documents, goes to the trustor's bank with the legal authority to transact on the personal checking account. Now, no gift has been made, everything is accounted for, and the trustor's wishes are fulfilled appropriately. Proper planning and then proper execution are good ways to reduce conflicts of interest.

Chapter 10
The Fraud Triangle

By *Jane B. Lorenz, CPA, CLPF (deceased)*:

I WAS SURPRISED AND PLEASED TO see "an old friend" written about in the Spring 2009 CAMICO IMPACT newsletter, as the "Fraud Triangle". I hadn't heard anyone beside myself refer to this "friend" since I left the University of Missouri as an Accounting graduate in 1968! The old friend I am referring to is the Fraud Triangle below...

NEED

OPPORTUNITY

JUSTIFICATION

I learned about this in my auditing training. There are three things necessary for theft (or fraud) to occur. One is NEED, the second is JUSTIFICATION and the third is OPPORTUNITY. Among our employees or service providers, we can be on the lookout for NEEDS, such as addiction and financial pressures. We can be alert for "justification" remarks that show that an employee is complaining about "fairness" and placing blame on others for his or her situation. And perhaps most importantly, we can make every effort to eliminate and minimize the opportunities for theft or fraud.

In a business, this is often referred to as INTERNAL CONTROLS. These are controls in place that makes it difficult for a single person to steal. A common example would be DIVISION OF RESPONSIBILITIES, such as assigning one person to open the mail and make a list of money received, another person to make the bank deposits, another person to prepare bank reconciliations. In the estate planning environment, when a single person is doing EVERYTHING, there is much opportunity for error, as well as for theft to occur. When the trustee is an inexperienced family member, the opportunities for error and for theft increase.

Among service providers, this would often be considered as AVOIDING CONFLICTS OF INTEREST. In the Estate Planning environment, a person that is the trustee and is also a beneficiary has a conflict of interest. A person who receives a commission on buys or sales has a conflict of interest if he/she is given the power to choose when and what to buy and sell. A person that receives a referral fee from a retirement facility has a conflict of interest when he/she has been asked to develop a discharge plan from a hospital.

So to consider the Fraud Triangle in relationship to choosing an inexperienced family member, the following issues might arise.

- **NEED**- the family member may have financial need (my daughter is ill" or "I need this money"). He/she may have vices (drinking, drugs, gambling).
- **JUSTIFICATION**-the family member may feel entitled ("they've given more money to my brother than to me," or "it's only temporary!" or "My sister thinks she's so smart!"
- **OPPORTUNITY**-the family member may have full access to cash on hand, valuable personal property or items easily

convertible into cash such as coins and diamonds. The family member may choose to not report to anyone. The family member may be adept at manipulating other family members.

What is Fraud?

Above we discussed elements that may cause stealing to happen. Fraud is a kind of theft. Theft in general is taking someone else's property. Embezzlement is taking funds which have been entrusted. Robbery is theft by force. Fraud has specific elements:

➢ **M**aterial (substantial)
➢ **I**ntentional (the perpetrator intends to deprive another)
➢ **L**ie (the victim was led to believe in a non-existent benefit)
➢ **K**nowing (the perpetrator knew he was telling an untruth)

Examples of fraud:

A caregiver comes to the elder and tells the story of a family member who needs surgery in the home country and must have $500 in cash today or the family member will die.

The elder receives an email (or phone call or letter) from someone claiming to be a grandson. His car has broken down and there is no way for him to get to school or work, could the elder mail him a money order right away (he has no checking account either).

The elder receives an email from the Canadian Lottery claiming that the elder has won $100,000 but must provide $8,000 up front to "pay the tax" before the money can be deposited in his account.

There is no defense against deceit. The Trustee must be on the lookout for questionable transactions and "gifts". A good estate plan, put into in action, can be an excellent prevention to elder financial abuse.

Chapter 11
Communication

THE PROBATE CODE IN SECTION 16060 "The trustee has a duty to keep the beneficiaries of the trust reasonably informed of the trust and its administration."

It has been our personal observation as human beings, that good Communication can be the most difficult thing! Even when loving people are taking full responsibility for themselves, it is challenging to communicate clearly.

Experience has taught us that written communication is vastly superior to other options. The writer is able to craft the choice of words in a quiet moment and review them before sending. The reader is able to read the words over and over again and to ask others for help in understanding. In later conversations, everyone can refer back to the written communication as a point in the flow of life. If new information becomes available, written communication can be modified by another written communication with a later date.

Many non-professionals are not in the habit of documenting conversations, the decision process, or responses to questions in writing. Note taking is tough during emotional conversations. Misunderstandings can flourish in that gap, and mistrust can accumulate. This seems to happen more often in situations with a painful history.

Beneficiaries vary so much in the way they receive new information, their expectations, their relationship with the family, the way they respond to "authority" and their willingness to cooperate. Add to this all the ways with which we can communicate with each other; cell phones, email, fax, letter, virtually, in person and telephone. After years of practice, regardless of which method the beneficiary chooses, we typically respond with a written letter, as described below.

A valuable technique for communicating with multiple remainder beneficiaries is to include all of their names in the greeting and address of every letter. It is then obvious that the trustee is communicating with everyone at once and every letter is the same. This ensures that there is not a subconscious worry that any beneficiary is being singled out by the trustee for good or bad treatment. We have also observed that often it is one beneficiary who asks the most questions, while other beneficiaries may be afraid to ask. This way of writing to the beneficiaries is a way of reassuring fairness while building trust.

The exception to this may be when the beneficiaries choose not to communicate with each other and therefore we cannot publish their mailing address to the others. When this is the case, we will use only their names, not the addresses on the letter itself, and individualize a cover letter to each one, informing them that the same letter has been published in the same way to each beneficiary.

When dealing with especially difficult communication (due to the nature of the news or the recipients), we draft this kind of letter, but have counsel be the one to send it out and receive responses. Sometimes we add a receipt to be signed and mailed back, if the communication has a deadline or decision to be made. We find working directly with our attorneys in these situations is typically more efficient.

Good communication not only benefits the recipients; good

communication can better protect the trust from the additional legal expenses of poor communication.

Amateur Fiduciaries (such as friends or family members) are often so caught up in the "upset" they do not fully consider their own protection, nor the way their actions will be assessed in the future, by the courts or others. In some families, "not speaking to each other" is a normal way to handle upset. The Trustee has the job of protecting the intentions of the trustor, accounting for every transaction, and making sure the administration is as efficient as it can be.

Trust accountings are a critical form of communication to both the trustor and beneficiaries. The accountings tell the story of the Trust and may be the only way for those involved to "see" the work of the trustee. As trustee, it is not enough to produce the accountings, but one must make sure that the appropriate parties have received their copy, in a timely fashion, and those same recipients are asked for their approval. Some trusts limit the "accounting objection period" to six months, or 180 days. When the document is silent on this (per California's Probate Code), or if a beneficiary objects to an item of the account in writing, beneficiaries have three years to object to the accounting. This is one of the reasons this aspect of the work should not be undertaken in a casual manner. Until approvals are acquired, or the accounting objection period has lapsed without any objections, the job of the trustee is not complete.

Many estate plans require at least an annual accounting, some require more frequent accounting. For many family member trustees, this is daunting in itself, as very few people actually account for their own spending in a detailed way. Typically, every bit of interest, every purchase, every stock sale or purchase in the portfolio, every bit of income, and more, are included in the accounting, resulting in dozens of pages of detail.

In addition to tracking every financial event, a good accounting also includes the values of any real property owned by the trust, along with accurate beginning and ending balances for every asset and account.

If you are going to serve as trustee, we strongly recommend

keeping track of all the transactions and the supporting information (such as receipts and invoices) from the very beginning of your service, guarding against any commingling of your personal funds with trust funds. We further recommend working closely with your attorney (and an experienced CPA) to make sure that expenditures are appropriate, and are following the trust distribution provisions closely.

When the matter is finally concluded, a final accounting will be necessary. There are factors that can make an accounting more complicated, such as the requirement to split certain expenditures into Principal and Income, explanations as to withdrawals from retirement accounts, business reporting, distributions based on percentages, and so on, requiring multiple schedules. Standard home accounting software does not usually have the tools needed to do a proper trust accounting either. Errors can result in the trustee being held personally liable, requiring repayment from personal funds.

The trustee has an affirmative duty to account, which makes the selection of the right trustee fundamental to the trust's success.

Chapter 12
Fairness to all Beneficiaries

ONE OF THE DUTIES OF the trustee is to be fair to all the beneficiaries. We discussed fair communication in Chapter 11. The fairness described here is in regard to the overall administration.

Probate Code Section 16003 reads:

"If a trust has two or more beneficiaries, the trustee has a duty to deal impartially with them and shall act impartially in investing and managing the trust property, taking into account any differing interests of the beneficiaries."

"Differing interests" may include the age of the beneficiaries. Investments often carry some form of risk. As an example, one might invest more aggressively for an 18-year-old than any 85-year-old. So a Trustee will need to consider the current and future needs/possibilities.

This is a particularly difficult duty to follow when the trustee is also a beneficiary. If the Trustee has always been told that Grandma's favorite pie plate is for her, how can she handle it when there are competing claims from her siblings for the same unique item?

How can the Trustee remain "fair" when he really feels that his brother has always been a "leech" on Mom and Dad? These are difficult ethical questions and families are often broken further apart by them. We have observed that the family dynamics don't go away as family's age.

Adult children are often "on their best behavior" while Mom and Dad are still alive. When Mom and Dad have died, childhood behaviors, reminiscent of the back seat of the car at age 5, often re-emerge. The "pecking order" may be re-established. Alliances of two against one may occur. A power struggle that has been growing for a lifetime may bloom! What chance does fairness have among beneficiaries in this environment? And so, the family structure takes a few more blows...and Thanksgiving together, may never be the same!

We have noticed that non-professional Trustees will often attempt to distribute assets in kind, as opposed to selling them and distributing cash. That can be messy when dividing lots of shares and having tiny amounts left over to sell. These same amateur fiduciaries may not discuss these details with an attorney until it is too late, because they don't understand that <u>doing what family members want is not the same as following the wishes of the Trustor</u>. And it can be truly unfair when attempting to divide indivisible things.

A few examples of indivisible things are:

- Mom's engagement and wedding rings
- Grandma's favorite pie plate
- The family home
- The family vacation home
- Dad's 1987 Corvette with very few miles on it.

Some families are able to come up with creative methods of distributing indivisible things like these. Some rotate ownership. What about insurance coverage and loss? Another ethical question is; what does the Trustor want to have done and can it be done in such a way as to benefit all of the beneficiaries? As the Trustee, one must look to the trust document (is equalization in distribution expected or is it expected that different beneficiaries will receive different amounts?) and focus on what the Trustor wanted to accomplish.

When the trust is silent or the instruction is something like, "all the children will share the personal property", family member trustees are truly challenged. Some compromise by each beneficiary getting their first choice with the choosing order determined by drawing names from a hat. Most people need an independent person or Trustee to handle that sort of process. Some may wish to seek court approval.

When families are really stuck, sometimes a professional Fiduciary, acting as Trustee and based on instructions in the trust document, can make the tough decision (like to sell a contended object and distribute the funds) or bring the proposed action to the court, with notice to all of the beneficiaries. The family members may all feel better about a professional carrying out such a task, where in cases in which the family member trustee did it, there would be war. Many professional fiduciaries train to be good at this kind of decision making and communication.

It has been our observation that the issues of personal property are often ignored until someone's feelings are hurt. We know of many estate planning attorneys who encourage their clients to make these decisions, before the plan is implemented. Unfortunately, many clients don't fill in the "Schedule A" or "Personal Property Distribution List" without prompting and encouragement. As professional Trustees, we make a point of visiting with the client/Trustor on this topic (whenever possible) before their plan must go into action, thereby supporting the plan drafted by the attorney. Very often, if a family member is named to serve in the future, the topic is volatile and goes unresolved during the life of the Trustor.

The elderly Trustor may not be willing to have a disagreement with the person they depend on for love and attention. Manipulation and control seeking are common in families. Independence is important and can be maintained without isolation. We encourage clients to visit with their attorney on a regular basis (every 2 or 3 years, depending on age) so that they develop a relationship, the clients can keep their plan up to date, and the attorney can refer them to assistance when the need arises. Ask your attorney, "Under what circumstances should I invoke my plan?"

Chapter 13
Notice to Heirs

THE PROBATE CODE PROVIDES THAT beneficiaries and legal heirs (who may not be named as beneficiaries in the Trust) be notified within 60 days of the death or other occurrence requiring the notification. For those non-professionals reading this, here is an example: You have decided to leave assets to two of your three children. Your third child hasn't spoken to you in years and you feel he doesn't need the money. Even though you have "written him out", as a "legal" heir, he is still entitled to "Notice".

Code section 16061.7 reads

"A trustee shall serve a notification by the trustee as described in this section in the following events:

1. When a revocable trust or any portion thereof becomes irrevocable because of the death of one or more of the settlors of the trust, or because, by the express terms of the trust, the trust becomes irrevocable within one year of

the death of a settlor because of a contingency related to the death of one or more of the settlors of the trust.

2. Whenever there is a change of trustee of an irrevocable trust. The duty to serve the notification by the trustee is the duty of the continuing or successor trustee, and any one co-trustee may serve the notification."

We think this procedure came into law around 1986 to respond to a particular concern. Apparently, there had been some cases where an elder acquired a new "friend" who became their beneficiary and perhaps their trustee as well. The elder died and the assets were distributed to the "new friend". Some time passed and it came to the attention of some family member who lived "back east" that the elder had died! They inquired, discovered the sequence of events and questioned its propriety. Unfortunately, the assets were gone. They had been spent.

So now, a formal notice is supposed to be sent to all those would inherit under state law if there were no trust. Initially, many attorneys and clients worried about this stirring up problems in the family and were resistive about following the new law. It appears now, most professionals feel that it is a good thing to get any "contests" into the light right away. It is likely that there will be documentation or memory of the reason behind any disinheritance, and it can be made apparent.

We encourage people who leave unequal distributions to siblings to write a letter to each one, explaining the reason and making it clear when this does not reflect a lack of love. Expressing love to beneficiaries is a very good thing to do. They want the money and many do equate money they receive from you with your love.

In a recent conversation with a "child" in his 60s, he revealed he is still hurting because his parents left him a lesser amount than to his sisters. He is a very well-educated person and he can imagine it probably had to do with "need" or "earning ability" but he confessed to a nagging fear that they loved him less. A loving letter could have eliminated such fears. We have seen it many times that the eldest, successful child has the responsibility to serve the parents through the end of life, because the other kids just can't. Then he acts as executor of the will, and per the trust, distributes more funds to his needy siblings than he is to receive because he doesn't "need" it. How would your family members feel?

We think it would be great if more people considered the affect this kind of process has on their family and then spoke to their attorney about alternatives.

Chapter 14
Personal Property

THINK ABOUT EVERYTHING PHYSICAL THING (your personal property) you own for a moment. Consider all the choices you made to select those particular items. Your reasons for selecting them are yours alone.

If you have any items you have received through inheritance, you may be keeping them because you enjoy them, or because you are holding onto them for the next generation. What items make you feel at home? What few things would you take with you if you moved to a smaller home, like an assisted living apartment?

For whoever serves as your Fiduciary, taking possession of personal property can be complicated and problematic. The Fiduciary's logical mind might ask "Why insist that this item go to a young person? They might not want it, or it isn't worth much! Compared to the other assets, it is of tiny value!"

That is often true. However, it is wise to assume that the personal property has significant sentimental value to someone in the matter. This means that emotions are attached, can erupt and even lawsuits can evolve out of those big emotions. A Fiduciary will often spend an inordinate amount of time and expense to handle personal property in deference to the possibility of those "big emotions". The emotions may not be "visible" until later and the distribution of personal property is often one of the first tasks the Fiduciary must complete. Often the home must be emptied right away (to be sold, or to avoid an additional month's rent). After the beneficiaries have received the items to which they are entitled, and the rest sold, there are often items left behind to be donated or thrown away.

One of the difficulties of handling personal property is that is usually unlisted and untitled. So the first task is to protect whatever there is from loss, damage or theft. That usually involves changing the locks on the property so that only the Fiduciary has access. The locksmith can often assist with other security matters like windows and doors.

Then the next task is to document whatever is there. Many Fiduciaries, when they become active as the Trustee, either photograph or videotape all of the personal property on their first visit. It creates a record of what was there at that moment in time. There are now professional inventory specialists who can create a catalogue, facilitate distribution, and help get information such as history and value. This is an extra expense, but often worth it. This means going through every square foot of the home; opening boxes in the garage, dresser drawers and all the cabinets.

If something is later missing, it may be possible to show that it was or was not there at the first visit. Because it is difficult to prove, it is recommended that a Fiduciary not enter a property alone before the personal property has been listed and quantified. It is wise to always have another staff member, a realtor, an appraiser, or a locksmith present when visiting the now vacant home filled with personal property. This reduces any possibility of theft, and provides assistance with the inventory process.

You may wonder why there is concern about theft? Your clients appointed you and trust you! That may be true but, family members and friends may have other points of view. It is not uncommon for elders to promise certain items of personal property to individuals!

They may have talked about it several times, but never wrote it down. If that item is not found among the personal property, the disappointed recipient may worry that it was stolen! You may never be able to satisfy that person but, you need to be able to establish if it was there when you took possession. You need to be able to say when the property was accessed and by whom. You don't want them to wonder if you favored one beneficiary over another or worse, took Grandma's' precious pie plate for yourself!

Some elders give things away to people who visit them. You don't want to be responsible for the items given away before you began your work as trustee. Elders/clients have the right to give things away and to choose their friends, and might not remember a long ago promise. The Fiduciary, and any other service provider, should never accept any gifts from the client, even though it is offered.

We have worked with many personal property appraisers. It is important to have a good inventory list, as well as having a fair, impartial value for the items. If the goal of the trust is to "equalize" distributions among beneficiaries, having a dollar value for each personal property item allows for proper accounting. For instance, your personal property is worth $10,000, and your whole estate is worth $100,000. You have four beneficiaries, and you would like them to each receive a quarter of your estate, valued at $25,000 each. 2 of your beneficiaries live far away, and they don't want any of the personal property. This leaves two beneficiaries who will receive some of your personal property. One beneficiary chooses one item worth $1000, and the other chooses to receive $4000 of personal property. The remaining personal property is sold, and the balance is added to the estate total which is then split 4 ways. The personal property amounts distributed to two of the beneficiaries are calculated in so that when all the distributions are completed, each of the four received equal shares.

The Trustee must follow the trust provisions regarding distributions. When creating your estate plan, please talk with your attorney about your personal property, and your expectations about what you think your beneficiaries want. Please don't expect your beneficiaries to agree. Please don't expect all of your beneficiaries to be all together in your home, at the same time, to "flip coins", or "draw straws". Please be mindful that your beneficiaries may not be able to even talk to each other at the time of distribution. It has been our experience, that when memorial gatherings are conducted in the home, some items mysteriously vanish.

We suggest listing a few specific items that you wish to distribute to specific beneficiaries, and allow your Trustee discretion as to the rest of your lifetime accumulation of stuff.

When you specify an item, like a piece of jewelry to go to a specific relative, please ask your attorney for an effective way to describe the item, its location, and provide photos to identify it, and paperwork that shows its value (like an appraisal).

If you have guns, please be specific with your attorney about your beneficiaries and your expectations. Even though you have identified a beneficiary doesn't mean that this beneficiary will be allowed to receive the gun if he/she does not pass required background checks.

When there are disputes between beneficiaries, there are hurt feelings, and there is often a great deal of time spent, both for the trustees and the attorneys involved, adding to the expense of administration. If you are inclined to share your bounty during your lifetime, you can give certain items to family members now, and enjoy the process.

Chapter 15
Compensation for the Trustee

A PPARENTLY, IN THE PAST, SOME attorneys served as trustees and took a "dual fee" for their services. Effective January 1, 1994 Probate Code Section 15687 provided that a trustee who is an attorney may receive only:

1. The Trustee's compensation provided in the Trust or
2. Compensation for legal services performed (unless approval for dual compensation is obtained

A waiver of this provision is considered "against public policy." Violation is grounds for discipline (Business and Professions Code Section 6103.6). So the taking "dual fees" of a trustee fee and a legal fee is now a legal decision as well as an ethical one.

As a general rule, Professional Fiduciaries do not discuss their fees with each other. It is my understanding that attorneys also avoid this discussion, as no one wants to be accused of "Price Fixing". We become aware of what other professionals charge when we contract with them.

We feel it is appropriate to discuss our fees with individual prospective clients, share our printed fee schedule and highlight different services we offer and when we would go to work for them (i.e., resignation, incapacity or death). Banks and Trust companies update their published fee schedules from time to time. At this writing, it seems most of these professions do not publish their rates on the internet, preferring to present their rates directly to potential clients. So, if you are a new professional, or an amateur, what do you charge?

Check into local court rules, ask your attorney, research as best you can, talk to other Fiduciaries, but ultimately, you have to decide for yourself. Consider your experience, availability, overhead, insurance costs, cost of living, and time. You may have to test your market by declaring your fee to a new prospect and gauging the response. Typically, amateurs get paid half of what corporate fiduciaries get paid because of their reliance on paid professionals and their lack of efficiency. In theory, less experienced attorneys get paid less than more experienced attorneys. The presumption is the more experience you have, the more efficient you are.

We cannot offer you a simple answer on this one, as we feel that this work is so complex, so laden with responsibility and so potentially risky in terms of litigation, you alone have to decide what you are willing to get paid to do this work. We update our fee schedule about every two years, or so, with careful consideration.

It is important that you feel you are being paid fairly for the work and risk involved. To be paid less may create unnecessary temptation; to be paid more may create the impression that you are taking advantage.

We feel good about our communication with our prospective and existing clients. We are clear with our clients and counsel about what we charge and discuss it before we go to work. In this way, knowing, voluntary and consensual contracts can be honored easily.

We are aware some family member trustees waive their fees. This work is not just a favor to a needy family member. This is a serious job that requires a great deal of time (often 3 years, or more), attention, liability, and decision making. Professionals have had years of training, are licensed, and insured. If you are to be compensated, you must track your time and your tasks. Be prepared to explain your tasks in terms of their benefit to the trust.

Chapter 16
Ethics in Action

A **BOUT THE FIRST TRUSTEE OF the Trust...**
This book has focused on those who serve as Successor Trustee, after the initial Trustee has become incapacitated, resigned or died. The Trustor (think "Employer") is often the first Trustee (think "Employee") of the Trust, and as such, has some significant responsibilities at the very beginning of the estate planning process.

The first job, after completion of the documents, is "Funding". In order for assets to be protected under the new Trust, they must be titled in the name of the Trust. Many attorneys assist the clients for whom they have prepared the trust documents in this important task. Real property, share ownership, bank accounts, investment accounts and other holdings often need a title update into the name of the Trust. Beneficiary designation forms may need to be updated, naming one's Trust as the beneficiary, rather than the names of individuals. Discuss this with your attorney to be sure that your funding efforts match your written plan.

Keeping track of what is in the Trust is another important job of the initial Trustee. Depending on the kind of trust and who serves as Trustee, there may be a new tax identification number, TIN, required, tax returns may need to be filed and all transactions documented. A husband and wife may be serving as "co-trustees" and there may be many decisions to be made when the trust begins. We recommend that everyone, especially those who are new to having a Trust of their own, work closely with their attorney to be sure they have satisfied all of the initial requirements and get training to maintain their Trust appropriately.

It seems that the most effective estate plans have been the result of creating a relationship with a qualified attorney who specializes in the area of estate planning. We suggest that you interview a few attorneys, to find the one with whom you feel the most comfortable. Know that you are embarking on a lifelong estate planning process, and your attorney is your guide and confidant. There will be changes in the law, changes in your relationships, and changes in your life which you will want reflected in your estate plan. Life's changes can be surprising. Recognize that your written plan is designed to change along with your life and having a good working relationship with an experienced attorney is a great way to keep your plan up to date.

Please note that in addition to maintaining the Trust appropriately, the Trustor has a responsibility to "think through" the management of the Trust, once the Trustor is no longer able to manage alone, in light of incapacity, resignation and death. Consider the conditions required for you to allow your successor trustee to begin working for you.

Here is a thought experiment to see if you have selected the right successor trustee. Give your checkbook to your selected person with only this instruction: "Pay my bills, on time, for the next two billing cycles". Will that person know what to do and where to find your important documents? How does this action make you feel?

We call the overarching process of trust management, "trust administration". Consider how your successor trustee will administer your trust, when the time comes. Will you feel comfortable enough to invoke your trust, if you become ill or weary? Will you actually let your Fiduciary go to work while you are alive? We hear from our colleagues that this is often a challenging discussion for the estate planning attorney to have with the client (the Trustor) who has already made so many decisions during the estate planning process. The attorney can suggest alternatives, but this choice is ultimately that of the Trustor.

Clearly, it is not just the documents as drafted, but as much the individual charged with the responsibility, that makes the difference in how a trust is administered. We feel this falls under Ethics for Trustees, as typically, the Trustor is not just the first Trustee of the Trust, but also the first beneficiary.

We respectfully suggest that our fellow professionals bring an "Ethics" discussion to the attention of the lay Trustor, to encourage successful administration of his/her goals and dreams. Ethically, the Trustor has a responsibility to choose well. Making good choices could mean the difference between family harmony and a family who never speak to each other again.

We offer four great questions to consider before selecting a Successor Trustee:

1. Does my successor trustee have experience and expertise in handling finances? Good accounting and bookkeeping skills? Trust and Estate tax experience?
2. Will my successor trustee remain objective, responsive and compatible with all beneficiaries of the trust and other members of the family?
3. Will my successor trustee be able to devote sufficient time to the management of the trust, unburdened by other obligations such as a job or a family, for three or more years?
4. Is my successor trustee also a beneficiary, causing a "Natural Conflict of Interest"?

If everyone considers the above questions, prior to making a decision, we feel that some of the courtroom volume will reduce, families will stand a better chance at continued peace, and fewer financial disasters will occur. Considering the effect of this extra work on a family member's busy life is a kind way to encourage success in the role as Trustee.

For those clients in their 40's, 50's and 60's, we suggest keeping your attorney up to date with your life by phone and meeting in person every 3-5 years. For clients who are 70 or better, updates/ meetings more frequently make sense, every 2-3 years. Let your attorney know your plan to stay up to date and discuss the cost of doing so. You could save your estate thousands of dollars by spending the money to have a well written and well maintained plan in the first place.

Chapter 17
Living as a Fiduciary

T HE CHALLENGES FOR AN INDEPENDENT Fiduciary are numerous. There are, potentially, so many people to serve and so many to report to. Days can be very long due to the emotional nature of the client circumstances (diminishing health, end of life issues, family dynamics...). If a Fiduciary neglects to rest, eat well and get some recreation, making good ethical decisions may be more difficult. Mindfulness takes practice and determination.

Mindfulness practice may include meditation, conscious breathing, long walks, journaling, etc. There are many ways to calm the mind and train it to focus on one thing at a time. Some use spiritual or religious practice to achieve inner quiet. We recommend that everyone who works as a Fiduciary find a mindfulness practice which feels natural and comfortable in order to have it at the ready for those expected challenges.

Think of delegation (allowing others to do some of the work, while supervising the outcome) as a way to protect you. If you are in the habit of delegating, it is more likely that your work, and its results, are transparent to the other professionals with whom you work. As in the discussion about how theft happens, there is less opportunity if more than one person knows what the bank balance should be. Collusion is much more difficult to achieve than individual theft.

An essential element of our Fiduciary practice is to have a professional investment advisor for each matter. Sometimes, the client already has a trusted advisor, with whom we then work. Some fiduciaries choose to manage all the investments, pay all the bills, transfer funds and document all the transactions alone. We feel that having another professional serve as custodian of the funds creates a natural check and balance system. The financial professional is in the business of tracking and understanding market fluctuations. This professional has extensive training on many more financial product options than we fiduciaries might have. When we request funds, we document what we receive and can then reconcile those requests against the record maintained by the custodian.

Delegation is helpful, but you may be the only one in the case to uphold high ethical standards. Other professionals, family members and even the client, may suggest shortcuts and "go arounds" that you know are questionable. This is when having good documentation habits can be critically important. Not only must you express the ethical standard, doing so in writing (as often as needed) can protect you later. Imagine writing every letter to, "Dear Jury". When writing, as if to a jury, you want to be clear on the facts and dates. You want your writing to be without bias. If you have to repeat yourself about the rules to particular beneficiaries, being consistent is easier to achieve in writing.

Some Fiduciaries feel they need to "do it all" themselves so they maintain control. They don't want to deal with partners, employees or having to explain everything. We certainly understand the desire to stay in control, however, we have seen a number of people, in a Fiduciary capacity, make critical mistakes, because they have avoided receiving help and avoided having others review their work. These are what we call, "Isolated Professionals".

Are you an "Isolated" professional? Have you insisted to others that you must do everything yourself or you will not have control? This is a great time to consider adjusting your approach so that; One, you can sustain your life and not burn out due to exhaustion and, Two, others can trust you more because you are sharing your work load appropriately and transparently.

There are lots of solutions that might help you maintain your high ethical standards and grow your practice. Some Fiduciaries have chosen to have part time help, use virtual office services or have a professional bookkeeper or CPA prepare their checks and accountings. This may mean sharing one's fees, but it also means one can take on more cases and vacations are possible.

Some days as a Fiduciary seem endless. Depending on the kind of service you offer, you could be at court in the morning and the hospital, visiting a client, in the afternoon. Many people may feel they have a right to your undivided attention. You must stay organized and protect your time, or you can become overwhelmed. Life as a sole proprietor has its challenges made exponential by serving in a highly ethical position such as a Fiduciary.

From an ethics standpoint, mindfulness and self-care are critical to success. It appears that stress (whether health, financial or social) contributes a great deal to poor decision making. Self-Care Choices to Consider:

Stress Relief – Do you have a "safe" person to discuss your cases with? Everyone needs a chance to process through his or her decision tree. Perhaps this is your attorney on that particular case. We meet with our staff every week regarding every case to be sure nothing goes without appropriate attention. We talk with each other so that our priorities stay clear. In this way, we receive and give assistance for the highest good of all concerned. COVID-19 has increased our need for regular communication and illustrates that obstacles can pop at any time, so we need to be ready to keep our well-oiled systems resilient.

Mindfulness – Is there a duty to be mindful? There are lots of demands on our time and attention; disappointed beneficiaries, resistant clients, serious deadlines, and so much more. Everyone benefits from a calm approach. With mindfulness we demonstrate our competence and diligence. When we come from a place of calm, others feel heard and accepted, and we learn more easily. We can receive new ideas and inspiration, without the clutter of worry or pessimism. Mindfulness makes our bodies feel better, and when we feel good, that overall sense of well-being helps to attract more of what we like. You can survive without Mindfulness, but thriving requires regular practice. When we practice Mindfulness, we give ourselves the opportunity to do our very best, regardless of our circumstances.

Health – Do you eat well? Are you getting enough rest? Are you taking time off to recreate? We deal with very serious topics every day, so vacation time is critical. As Fiduciaries, we are often exposed to those that are ill or prone to infection. We too need regular medical care. If you are the only one who can sign checks or make decisions, what do you do when you take a few days off? Developing a vacation plan is a good way to reduce stress.

Personal Finances – Do you have enough? What does abundance mean to you? How do you cope with the moments when it seems like you do not have enough? Many people have difficulty being honest with themselves in terms of what they have and what they want. The Chapter, "Compensation for the Trustee" is worth exploring so that you are paid adequately. People who feel cheated may not make good financial and ethical decisions.

Estate Planning – Is your personal estate plan up to date? Does your plan include what to do about your clients' needs, if something happens to you? Having successors named after you in the estate plans of your clients is just one piece. Knowing the court will replace you as conservator can be reassuring. Do you have a succession plan for your practice? Does your successor know where and how to access your client files? Will there be funds enough to keep things going long enough for your successors to take over, and might your successors be grieving their loss of you? Consider working with a business law attorney to tighten up your business planning, and then consider having your estate planning attorney and business law attorney talk with each other in order to protect you and the future of your clients, as best you can.

Continuing Education – The requirements for licensing in California include 15 hours of continuing education per year. Whether or not you are a professional, this is an obvious personal benefit in that there is so much to learn (legal, financial, tax and medical). We make an effort to meet some of the other people at all of the continuing education opportunities we attend in-person and virtually. You can get relevant, timely continuing education online, by joining other associations and from certain industry periodicals. You will have to determine which classes fulfill your licensing and membership requirements. We believe no education is wasted.

Staying strong takes focus, setting good priorities and reducing your stress. Keep in mind, good character is demonstrated by what we do when we know no one is watching. The challenges we work through give us opportunities to keep improving internally and externally. We see the choices our clients make up close, and a smart Fiduciary is a lifelong student who learns from every matter.

This work is not for everyone. It is certainly the most challenging work of my career. I have had to use everything I have ever learned and I continue to learn new things with every case. As my Dad said many times, "We don't get paid to wash clean dishes…" I love this work, being of service to others and the satisfaction that comes at the close of every case.

I continue to follow advice I received from an attorney friend many years ago, "When a mistake happens, confess it immediately and fix it as soon as you can." If you consider every facet, take good notes, take care of yourself and plan "with the end in mind", you will be successful and happy in your Fiduciary life.

In the last few weeks of Jane's life, I asked her for whatever advice she wanted to give. She said, "Love as much as you can".

We like Rotary's Four-Way Test:
1. Is it the TRUTH?
2. Is it FAIR to all concerned?
3. Will it build GOODWILL and BETTER FRIENDSHIPS?
4. Will it be BENEFICIAL to all concerned?

Whatever your personal process to stay in touch with your values, surround yourself with good people, keep reading and continue to love and learn all you can.